The Basic Essentials of
Edible Wild Plants
& Useful Herbs

By Jim Meuninck

Illustrations by
Peggy Duke

ICS BOOKS, Inc.
Merrillville, Indiana

THE BASIC ESSENTIALS OF EDIBLE WILD PLANTS & USEFUL HERBS

Published by:
ICS Books, Inc.
One Tower Plaza
107 E. 89th Avenue
Merrillville, IN 46410

LIBRARY OF CONGRESS
Library of Congress Cataloging-in-Publication Data

Meuninck, Jim, 1942-
    Edible wild plants & useful herbs : the basic essentials / by Jim
Meuninck ; illustrations by Peggy Duke.
      p.   cm.
    Includes index.
    Bibliography: p.
    ISBN 0-934802-41-6 : $4.95
    1. Wild plants, Edible--United States--Identification. 2. Wild
plants, Edible--United States--Therapeutic use. 3. Wild plants,
Edible--United States--Pictorial works. 4. Cookery (Wild foods)
I. Title. II. Title: Edible wild plants and useful herbs.
QK98.5.U6M48 1988
581.6'32'0973--dc 19   8β-13354
                                                              CIP

TABLE OF CONTENTS

Introduction

Basic Essentials of Edible Wild Plants is a lifetime of experiences put to pen, experiences gained over the past 30 years foraging for edible and medicinal wildflowers in the United States, Japan, China, Europe and Canada. This record, however, is not new. Our ancestors, clad in animal skins, began this record thousands, perhaps millions of years ago. By trial and error, they discovered which plants were edible and which plants were poisonous. Modern studies by anthropologists around the globe suggest that eating wildflowers may have numerous benefits beyond good taste. The 100 plus Paleolithic plants described in this book are high in fiber, high in calcium, full of vitamins and minerals but low in fat. Many of these plants contain healthful Omega-3 fatty acids, whereas most cultivated vegetables lack these vital oils. Wild plants are genetically pure — natural foods, containing essentially complete germ plasma untampered by human hands. Yes, our ancestors implore us to consider the original foods evolution programmed us to eat.

So let's begin our walk back through time along the tangled and twisted paths of our ethnobotanical heritage. The trail will uncover authoritative, practical tips on gathering, preparing and cultivating edible wild plants. Learn how to prepare herbal teas. Uncover wild flower salad recipes. Discover folk remedies. American Indian uses and Chinese pharmaceutical uses of wildflowers. Learn your berries, and how to make berry-delicious desserts. Here and there along the path, modern pharmaceutical uses are uncovered. Topnotch companion books are identified.* Wildflower seed sources are surveyed. Where appropriate there are wildflower gardening tips. Poisonous plants are attended to. All recipes are proven, from my 30 years of experience, and the vast human record that goes before me.

The book is organized somewhat differently than traditional field guides. Most books structure content by season, or flower color. I have chosen to identify plants as you would stumble across them walking in a woods, trekking through a meadow, or paddling through a marsh. This practical approach begins with the familiar and progresses to unfamiliar, exotic species. the story opens in Painter Marsh ... a typical wetland, harboring edible, water loving flora.

*Recommended Reading: *Wild Foods,* Roger Phillips, Little, Brown ... *The Paleolithic Prescription,* Shostak, et. al., Harper & Row.
**Plants in this book can be found in the contiguous United States.

Wild Plant Foraging Rules

1. Before eating any wild plants study with an expert. Or take the plant to an expert for positive identification. Always cross reference with two or more field guides. Make certain you have seen color photos of the plants, black and quite photos, or illustrations in this book are not sufficient for positive identification.
2. After positive identification of an edible plant, taste only a very small amount of it. This precaution may protect you from allergic reaction or misidentification.
3. Beware of the carrot family: Hemlock, Waterhemlock and other members of this family are extremely poisonous Learn to distinguish Hemlock and Waterhemlock from Elder (elderberries).
4. Jim Meuninck does not endorse herbal medication, self diagnosis or self medication. The pharmaceutical references in this book are descriptions from what I have read. Please do not self-medicate. Seek consultation from your physician.
5. Practice conservation. Never collect more plants than you intend to use. Do not pick rare or endangered species. Work with a professional botanist to restore wild plants from areas where they have disappeared.
6. Avoid harvesting plants from polluted ground. Plants growing along roads may be tainted with benzene, lead, oil and other auto pollutants. Plants dwelling in streams and along fields near farms may be polluted with herbicides and pesticides ... Forage carefully. Droppings from wild game may spread bacteria, viruses, worms, giardia, amoebas and other forms of contamination into water nurturing wild edible plants. BE CAREFUL! Wash and cook all plants foraged from wild lands.

Editor's Note: This book is designed to be used with Jim Meuninck's 60 minute video, <u>Edible Wild Plants.</u> The numbers in parentheses next to each plant's genus species is the location of each plant on the video. Use your counter to locate the approximate position of an individual plant. ICS hopes the use of these numbers will make it easier to use the book with the video.

Rivers, Lakes, Ponds & Swamps

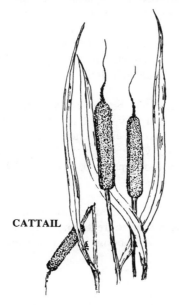

CATTAIL

BROAD LEAF CATTAIL (Typha latifolia)
NARROW LEAF CATTAIL (Typha angustifolia)

DESCRIPTION: Worldwide range. Long, sword-shaped leaves; green flowers on tandem spikes, lower spike female, upper spike male. There are two species of cattails common to North America: broad leafed and narrow leafed. The major difference is in the wideness of the leaf.

Cattails are a versatile foodstuff. The roots, new shoots and flowering heads are edible. In the spring, simply find the shoots*, reach down into the mud and pull. Peel off the outer leaves and underneath is the tender tongue of cattail. Saute this delicate core for three to five minutes in butter. Season with a few drops of soy sauce, and a pinch of wild ginger.

*Caution: Before eating Cattail shoots learn to distinguish young Cattail shoots from the poisonous look-alike Iris shoots.

A bit deeper in the soil is the long root where the cattail was attached. The root core is an excellent source of starch. Eat the starch raw as quick energy food. Or better yet, crush the roots in cold water and leach out the starch. The starch may be added to soups and stews as a thickener.

About mid-June, the male flowering head of the cattail, located above the female flower spike, may be stripped into a plastic bag. This high protein flour extender will keep in your freezer for 8 months ... Or use it immediately.

PREPARATION: Add the male parts, the pollen, anthers and stamens, to your favorite pancake mix. About one cup of cattail parts to two cups of mix. Also, try pollen and male parts mixed with flour — in cookies, muffins, biscuits and bread recipes.

The young female bloom spike may be cooked like corn-on-the- cob. Simply boil or steam the female spike in lightly salted water. Cook till tender. Butter and eat hot. Very young spikes may be eaten uncooked.

Cattail pollen may be mixed with raw honey, 5 parts cattail pollen to one part honey. This is high energy food, quick to prepare and has a long storage life if refrigerated below 40 degrees F.

PHARMACEUTICAL USES: Without endorsing herbal medicine, I've discovered cattail parts have been used to treat gonorrhea, worms, and diarrhea ... The chopped root is also applied to burns and minor cuts. The Chinese use the plant to stop bleeding.

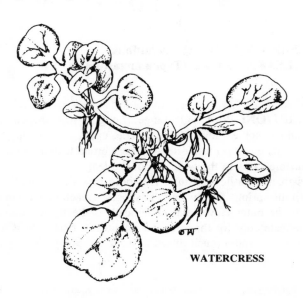

WATERCRESS

WATERCRESS (Nasturtium officinale) (091)

DESCRIPTION: Grows in shallow, clean water; alternate leaves, leaves to ¾" in width, ovate, simple, broad near base; small white flower with 4 petals. Avoid contamination from pesticides and herbicides. Collect watercress (and for that matter all edible water plants) from a clean water source: A highland stream or free flowing spring.

Watercress is a pungent spicy green, an important ingredient in V8 cocktail juice, and one of the most useful greens known to humankind. In the northern tier of states and Canada, watercress is available 10 months a year. South of the Mason Dixon line it's a year around food.

COOKING TIPS: Scramble chopped watercress with eggs ... Stuff a PITA sandwich. Saute it ... add it to salads, or make watercress soup.

ONE FAVORITE RECIPE is smoked bass stuffed with watercress. After washing the body cavity, stuff the fish with watercress. Season to taste. Then bake or smoke the fish.

It's a good idea to cook all watercress gathered from the bush, because of possible contamination. I like to stir fry watercress with a tablespoon of oil, two tablespoons of soy sauce and the juice of one garlic clove. Cook briefly at medium heat for about two minutes.

PHARMACEUTICAL USES: Watercress is high in Vitamins C and A. It is a mild diuretic. A few Indian groups used watercress to dissolve gallstones.

DUCKWEED (Spirodela polyrhizd) (117)

DESCRIPTION: One or two 3/16" oval leaves. Threadlike root hairs. Floating, hydroponic plant. You've probably seen duckweed. It's the green slime completely covering ponds in mid- summer. Upon closer inspection, the green water cover is one of the smallest flowering plants. This plant is hydroponic, the tiny root hairs siphon nutrients from the water.

COOKING TIPS: Duckweed is edible. Intrepid foragers may blend it into their favorite soup recipe. More conservative folks use it sparingly — duckweed has an unusual, tough texture, pleasing to some, distasteful to others. *Like all wild plants, use this plant sparingly. If you have any food allergies, be especially careful.*

PHARMACEUTICAL USES: The Chinese use duckweed to treat hypothermia, flatulence, and acute kidney infections.

REED GRASS

REED GRASS (Phragmites communis) (134)

DESCRIPTION: Tall wetland grass; lance shaped leaves up to 1' in length, flowers in tall dense plume, plants grow in dense cluster. Reed grass is found around the margins of streams and in wet lowlands. The root of reed grass, like cattail roots, may be harvested, and leached of its starch.

COOKING TIPS: The first shoots of spring may be eaten raw, but are best steamed until tender. Prepare the plant immediately after picking, delays in preparation make for a tough, stringy meal. Simply chop the new shoots to a manageable size. Place them in a steamer. They are ready to eat in 5 minutes. In the fall, seeds may be stripped, crushed and cooked with berries. Or ground into flour. Also, try reed seeds cooked in stews and soups.

PHARMACEUTICAL USES: Chinese use this plant to clear fevers, quench thirst, promote diuresis and promote salivation.

WILD RICE

WILD RICE (Zizania aquatica) (144)

DESCRIPTION: Tall, reedlike grass; long, narrow leaf blades, flowers in tall plume, upper flowers female, lower flowers male. Wild rice is a tall grass found growing in shallow, clean water. The seeds may be harvested in August and September. Timing is critical. Check your stand of wild rice often. Mature seeds drop off easily. Return every other day to maximize the harvest.

To thresh the husks from the seed use a rolling pin. Simply roll back and forth over the grain. Use a fan or the wind to dispel the chaff.

COOKING TIPS: The simplest way to cook wild rice is boil 2 cups of water, lightly salted, enter a cup of wild rice, cover and simmer for 35 minutes. Makes an excellent stuffing for wild turkey. Extend your supply by cooking it half and half with long grained brown rice.

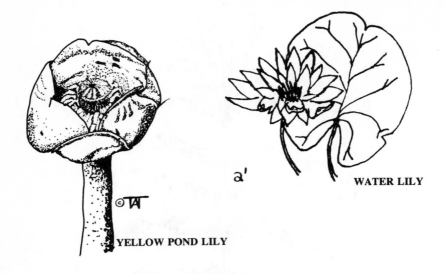

WATER LILY

YELLOW POND LILY

YELLOW POND LILY, SPATTERDOCK (Nuphar variegatum) (174)

DESCRIPTION: Disk shaped leaf, unfurls above water; yellow flower. The yellow flower blooms through the summer, bearing a primitive looking fruit. The fruit pod contains numerous seeds, perhaps the only palatable part of this plant. The root stock of spatterdock may be cut free and boiled. It smells sweet like an apple, but it's a bitter pill to swallow — even after cooking in 2 or 3 changes of water. Strictly a survival food, when nothing else is available.

COOKING TIPS: The seeds may be dried and ground into flour, or prepare them like popcorn. Place the dried seeds in a popcorn popper. Cover the machine so the small seeds don't become airborne. The results are usually disappointing. Seeds simply pop open. But they're edible with salt and butter.

FRAGRANT WATER LILY (Nymphaea odorata) (193)

DESCRIPTION: Large platter shaped leaves that float flat, 6" to 10" in diameter; large white flower. The white flowered, fragrant water lily, with its flat platter-like leaves, is edible. This beautiful waterplant is simple to transplant. Place it in a clay pot submerged in fresh water.

COOKING TIPS: Pioneers ate the unfurled leaves, and the unopened flower buds. The flower petals may be eaten with salad greens.

PHARMACEUTICAL USES: Dried root used to treat mouth sores, astringent.

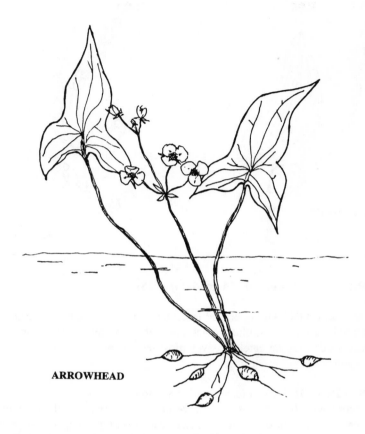

ARROWHEAD

ARROWHEAD, WAPATO (Saggitaria latifolia) (215)

DESCRIPTION: Arrow shaped leaves, veins palmate; white flower, three platter-shaped petals. Arrowhead (also called wapato) has an edible tuber attached to its root. The plant looks similar to poisonous arrow arum. To avoid confusing the two, note: arrowhead leaves are palmate — that is, all veins run out from a single source like fingers on the palm of a hand. Whereas, arrow arum has pinnate veins, veins that run out along the entire length of the mid-rib vein that dissects the leaf.

COOKING TIPS: The arrowhead tuber may be harvested in the fall, winter, or spring. Boil the tuber till tender. Remove the peel, mash the contents in a frying pan, cook like hashbrowns.

PHARMACEUTICAL USES: Amerindians used the root to treat tuberculosis. Root used internally to treat fever.

PICKERAL WEED

SWAMP DOCK

PICKERAL WEED (Pontederia cordata) (226)

DESCRIPTION: Arrow shaped leaf, veins spread from base, merge at tip like venation in grass leaves, blue flowers, densely clustered spike. Young leaves and mature seeds may be eaten. Leaves most tender in spring, while unfurling beneath water.

COOKING TIPS: Cook leaves with dandelions and mustard greens. Season cooked greens with Italian dressing. Serve hot. Add flower petals to salads. In late summer, seeds mature in tough, leathery capsules. Open capsule to get fruit. Munch as a trail food, or dry and grind into flour.

SWAMP DOCK (Rumex verticillatus) (230 +)
SOUR, CURLED DOCK (R. crispus)
YELLOW DOCK (R. obtusifolius)

DESCRIPTION: Broad lance shaped leaves, sometimes curled; smooth long stems; green flowers clustered on stalks; many seeds. Swamp dock is found in wetlands. Tender young leaves, as they emerge, are most edible. Older leaves tough and inedible. Sour dock, the preferred plant, is found on higher ground, fields, wasteland. Dock seeds are edible in late summer and autumn.

PHARMACEUTICAL USES: Sour dock roots used as a laxative. Root also used with vinegar to treat ringworm. Swamp dock used unsuccessfully to treat smallpox.

WILD ROSE

AMERICAN ELDER

WILD ROSE (Rosa spp.) (234)

DESCRIPTION: Bush; spiny branches; white, pink or red flowers, leaves alternate, compound, sharply toothed margins. Common edible found along the margins of waterways. There are several species of wild rose. Flowers give rise to the famous fruit, rose hip ... An excellent source of Vitamin C, available autumn.

COOKING TIPS: Rose petals and rose leaves may be dried and used for tea. Petals are a sweet, aromatic, add to summer floral salads.

PHARMACEUTICAL USES: Excellent Vitamin C source ... Used to prevent scurvy. The Chinese and Amerindians used rose tea to treat worms and intestinal disorders.

AMERICAN ELDER, ELDERBERRY (Sambucus canadensis) (240)

DESCRIPTION: Shrub; leaf feather-like, compound, 11 + - leaflets, toothed; white flowers in dense, flat or rounded cluster. American elder thrives along the edges of streams, bogs and other wetlands. The summer flowers may be batter fried, or eaten raw. But be cautious, learn to distinguish elder flowers from poisonous water Hemlock flowers ... *Use a field guide and forage with a knowledgeable botanist. Make positive, expert identification. Cross reference with two or three field guides ... Make certain you have seen color photos of the two plants.*

COOKING TIPS: Elderberry matures in late summer, and may be boiled into a fruit drink, made into jelly, or fermented into wine ... My favorite recipe is elderberry/apple pie ... You'll need: 2 cups of elderberries; 1 cup of blackberries or, a cup of wild grapes. Mix berries with 2 cups of cooking apples. Stir in 3 tablespoons of brown sugar or maple syrup. Add: teaspoon of cinnamon; half teaspoon of nutmeg; and 1 egg. Pour the contents into a pie shell. Sprinkle a pinch of flour over each layer. Place several pats of butter over the filling. Cook pie topless (325F) or cover with a crust.

North American Berries

WILD STRAWBERRY

STRAWBERRY (Fragaria virginiana) (285)

DESCRIPTION: White flower, sharply toothed leaflets, in threes. Wild strawberries may be found in meadows and open woods. Harvest in late May and early June.

COOKING TIPS: A favorite strawberry recipe combines one whole seedless orange, peel and all with cup of strawberries, cup of blackberries or mulberries. Add: an egg, half cup of vegetable oil. Blend ingredients. Then mix cup and half flour with with ¾ cup of sugar, teaspoon of baking powder, teaspoon of baking soda, and teaspoon of salt. Add half cup of raisins and cup of black walnuts. Make large muffins. Bake at 375 degrees for about 20 minutes. Here's all the energy and protein you need to kick off a day.

Remember, most berries, even rose hips, may be used in this recipe.

PHARMACEUTICAL USES: Tea mildly astringent. Fruit used as folk remedy for gout, Vitamin C treatment for scurvy.

11

RASPBERRY

BLACKBERRY

RASPBERRY (Rubus idaeus, R. occidentalis) (309)

DESCRIPTION: Shrub; compound leaves, 3-5 leaflets, sharply toothed, white flowers, 3 or more petals, spiny branches. Red and black raspberries are found along the fringes of woods, fence rows and the margins of fields. Berries are ready for harvest in late spring and early summer.

COOKING TIPS: Use as pie filling (see elderberry-apple pie recipe). Or stir into pancake batter and muffin mixes. Makes excellent jam or jelly. Also, use as substitute for strawberries in muffin recipe mentioned above.

PHARMACEUTICAL USES: Leaves are steeped in tea, a tonic for pregnant women. Amerindians used root for diarrhea, dysentery. Also, used to flavor medicines.

BLACKBERRY (Rubus allegheniensis) (318)

DESCRIPTION: Similar to raspberry; shrub, spiny branches, compound leaves, 5 + - leaflets, toothed, white flower bloom appears after raspberries. Blackberries are often found near your raspberry source. There are several species. Blackberries ripen in mid and late summer.

COOKING TIPS: Here's a low calorie, high nutrition breakfast made with raspberries or blackberries ... or both. Mix 2 cup of berries with two cups of low fat, sweetened vanilla yogurt. Add a dash of milk, and blend ... A wonderful ice cream substitute with only half the sugar and fat. Also, use in pies, muffins, pancakes, jellies and jams. Make tea from leaves.

PHARMACEUTICAL USES: Amerindians used roots with other herbs for eye sores, back ache and stomach ache. Pioneers made blackberry vinegar to treat gout and arthritis. Chinese use Rubus tephordes in a tea to stimulate circulation ... They claim it helps alleviate pain in muscles and bones.

BLUEBERRY (Vaccinium spp.) (328)

DESCRIPTION: Shrub; leaves alternate, simple, smooth margin, flowers white to pink, tightly clustered. Blueberries are available from early summer through early autumn. There are several species found in highlands, lowlands, openlands and wooded areas.

COOKING TIPS: For a simple blueberry treat, pour a bowl of FROZEN blueberries. Cover with Half and Half, whole milk ... or low fat milk. This frozen dessert sets up quickly and is ready to eat. A refreshing, cooling, low sugar, world class treat. Use blueberries pies, pancakes and other fruit recipes covered in this book.

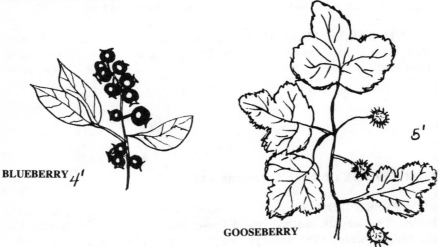

BLUEBERRY 4'

GOOSEBERRY

5'

GOOSEBERRY and CURRANT (Ribes spp.) (340)

DESCRIPTION: Shrub; spiny branches, gooseberry fruit is spined, currant smooth or spined fruit, deeply lobed leaves, sharply toothed, flowers yellow, purplish, white depending on species. In woodlands, and along the margins of woods you may find gooseberries and currants. There are several species. Spiny, dangerous looking, but harmless berries are ready for harvest in mid-summer.

COOKING TIPS: Make gooseberry/currant pie from elderberry pie recipe. Be certain to add lemon juice to punch up the taste.

PHARMACEUTICAL USES: Gooseberry and currant made into a jelly, spiced with peppermint, lemon juice and ginger ... Then taken as a sore throat remedy. Others claim (unsubstantiated by author) that Gamma-Linolenic Acid (GLA) an active ingredient of currants, may prevent acne, obesity and schizophrenia.

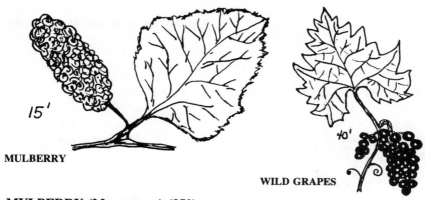

15'

MULBERRY

WILD GRAPES

40'

MULBERRY (Morus spp.) (350)

DESCRIPTION: Small tree; leaves simple, alternate, toothed, round or slightly elongated, broadest near base, flowers green, tiny, clusted on spike. Not far from gooseberries are mulberries. Mulberry trees found along roads, the fringes of woods, fence rows, and about anywhere berry-eating birds have re-distributed the seeds. There are red, white and black varieties. Do not eat the unripened fruits and leaves because they are slightly hallucinogenic. But ripened fruits are very edible.

COOKING TIPS: Mulberries, gooseberries and currants may be combined or used separately to make fudge. Gently cook cup and half mulberries until hot. Mash berries through a fine sieve to separate the juice. Mix in 2 cups of sugar. Add 3 tablespoons of butter. Re-heat slowly to dissolve butter. Bring to boil over medium heat. Do not stir. Let the mixture form a hot soft ball between 235 and 240 degrees F. on a candy thermometer. Cool till warm, then whip the mixture with a wood spoon for a few seconds. Press the fudge into a buttered pan, and cut pieces. Eat immediately or cover and refrigerate. The candy has a stringy, taffy-like consistency, messy to eat ... When serving kids, have lots of room and sufficient water.

PHARMACEUTICAL USES: Botanists say mulberry leaves and unripened fruits have mild sedative effect. Ripe fruit cooked with sugar and mixed with vodka has a stimulating effect (short lived I'll bet).

WILD GRAPES (Vitis spp.) (370)

DESCRIPTION: Climbing vine, clinging tendrils, green flowers in a large cluster; leaves alternate, simple, round, toothed, heart shaped base. The young leaves and ripe fruits are edible. They are found nationwide clinging and climbing trees, walls, and fences. The Canadian Moonseed plant looks like wild grape, but is poisonous. Learn to distinguish these two plants before eating what you think is wild grapes. Get expert identification.

COOKING TIPS: Wild grapes may be dried in sun for three days to make raisins. Cover the grapes with cheesecloth to keep flies off. Also, grapes may be used in elderberry pie mentioned earlier. Grape leaves are wrapped around rice, vegetables and meat. Steam stuffed leaf till tender. Add grape leaves to pickling spices when preparing dill pickles.

PHARMACEUTICAL USES: Grapes, the fruit, leaves and tendrils, have been used by Amerindians and pioneers to treat hepatitis, diarrhea, snakebite. Amerindians used tonic made with grape and several other herbs to increase fertility.

SUMAC

WINGED SUMAC (Rhus copallina) (380)
STAGHORN SUMAC (R. typhina) (384)

DESCRIPTION: Shrub, or small tree; leaves lance shaped, alternate, compound, numerous leaflets, toothed, cone-shaped flower and berry clusters. The large berry spikes of staghorn sumac are ready to harvest in late summer.

COOKING TIPS: Strip red berries of staghorn sumac from heads. Discard stems and heads. Soak cotton-covered berries in hot water to extract a lemonade-like drink. Steep sassafras root in the tea. Add sugar and serve.

PHARMACEUTICAL USES: Staghorn sumac flower has been steeped into tea, and taken for stomach pain. Gargles made from berries purported to help sore throats.

Yards and Meadows

DANDELIONS

DANDELIONS (Taraxacum officinale) (400)

DESCRIPTION: Flower heads yellow; leaves irregular, sharply lobed, in basal whorl, large taproot. Leaves, crown, roots and flower petals are edible. The seeds are a favorite food of goldfinch. Dandelion leaves are best in early spring before they flower. Older, bitter leaves may be improved by soaking them for an hour or so in a bowl of water with a teaspoon or so of baking soda mixed in. Dandelion leaves are high in Vitamins A, C, and B1.

COOKING TIPS: Favorite dandelion recipe goes like this: Chop 2 handfuls of dandelion leaves. Mix this with ¼ cup chopped nuts ... Your choice. Add juice of half lemon or lime. Blend in three tablespoons of honey with one teaspoon of olive oil. Mix ingredients well. Here's a meal full of vitamins and quick energy.

Also, use dandelion flowers in tossed salads. The crown of the plant, the whitish area just below the leaves and above the roots, may be deep fried. First, coat crowns in tempura batter. Then deep fry ... Try it! You'll be glad you did.

Dandelion coffee may be made from the root. Let the root dry in a warm dry place. Then roast the root lightly. Grind the root to powder. Add one teaspoon of powder to cup of hot water. Here's a bitter tonic that may be good for the liver.

PHARMACEUTICAL USES: Dandelion tea, made from roots, was used as laxative, blood purifier, and diuretic. For 5000 years dandelion parts have been used to clear fevers, break up congestion and stimulate milk flow in nursing mothers. Recent evidence suggests dandelion tea may rejuvenate alcoholics' liver.

17

CHICKWEED

CHICKWEED (Stellaria spp.) (426)

DESCRIPTION: Leaves oval, ¼" to ½"; stem weak, hairy, prostrate, ½" flower white, 10 + - lance shaped petals. Chickweed, a common ground cover, may be eaten raw or cooked.

COOKING TIP: Sprinkle chickweed flowers in with leaves when preparing a salad. Stew chickweed with rabbit, chicken, or beef. Add 4 cups flowers, leaves and stems to pot. Mix in favorite stewing herbs. Enter bird, bunny, or beef. Then brace yourself for a magnificent feast.

Chickweed pancakes: Blanch cup of chickweed for three minutes. Then chop leaves in a blender. Add blended greens to pancake batter. Later in the year, when the seeds mature, they may be used to thicken soup. Seeds excellent bird feed.

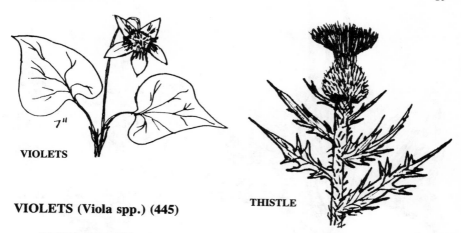

VIOLETS

THISTLE

VIOLETS (Viola spp.) (445)

DESCRIPTION: Flower irregular; leaves vary, usually ovate, common blue violet has heart shaped leaves, serrated. Found along fringes of lawn, in shady areas. Violets are cultivated in France for perfume. This incredible edible is high in Vitamin C and A.

COOKING TIPS: Use both the leaves and flowers in salads. Flowers may be candied. Whip powdered sugar with one egg white. Dip flower heads in sugared egg white, deep fry in a wok.

WARNING: LATE SEASON PLANTS WITHOUT FLOWERS MAY BE CONFUSED WITH INEDIBLE GREENS. FORAGE THIS PLANT ONLY WHEN IN BLOOM.

PHARMACEUTICAL USES: Violet roots consumed in large amounts are emetic and purgative. Plant used as poultice over skin abrasions. Chinese Barefoot doctors use one species, Viola diffusa, to treat aplastic anemia, leukemia, mastitis, mumps and poisonous snake bites.

BULL THISTLE (CIRSIUM VULGARE) (452)

DESCRIPTION: Thorny biennial, flower purple rises from spiny bract. Barbed leaves of the first year's growth may be eaten after the spines have been stripped away with a knife.

COOKING TIPS: Wear gloves when harvesting roots and leaves. Strip armor away from leaves with knife, eat raw or cooked. Flavor similar to celery. Harvest leaves in the spring and fall. In summer, flower petals may be sprinkled over salads. Roots may be boiled, sliced and stir fried. Some folks steam outer green bract around flower heads and eat bract like artichokes.

PHARMACEUTICAL USES: Chinese use thistle teas and decoctions to treat appendicitis, internal bleeding, and inflammations.

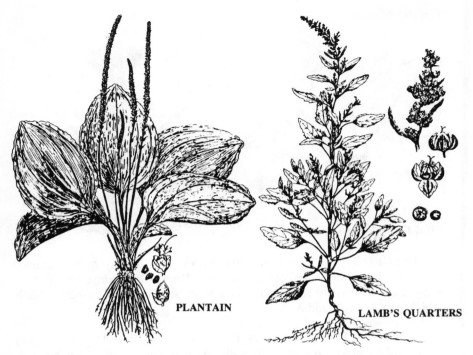

PLANTAIN

LAMB'S QUARTERS

PLANTAIN, BUCKHORN (Plantago major) (P. lanceolata) (470)

DESCRIPTION: Flowers green, tiny, numerous on spike; ovate leaf with pointed tip. Lanceolata has lancelike leaves, longer spike. Plantain is best harvested before this flower stalk appears. New leaves keep coming all year.

COOKING TIPS: Use young, tender leaves in salads. Soak older leaves in dilute salt water for ten minutes, then steam till tender. Dried seeds may be eaten whole or ground into flour.

PHARMACEUTICAL USES: One over-the-counter laxative uses seeds from the psyllium species of plantain. Barefoot doctors use whole plant as tea to clear fever and promote healing.

LAMB'S QUARTERS (Chenopodium album) (480)

DESCRIPTION: Lamb's quarters may be found in fields, on waste ground, and in just about everyone's garden. A healthy lamb's quarters plant may climb three feet tall. But it's the young tender leaves and tips that produce the best salad greens.

COOKING TIPS: As pot herb, boil lamb's quarters for 5 minutes with mustard greens and dandelion leaves. For a nutritious snack add seeds to your favorite bread or muffin mix.

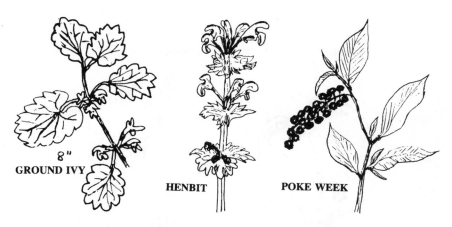

GROUND IVY   HENBIT   POKE WEEK

GROUND IVY, GILL-OVER-GROUND (Glechoma hederacea) (498)

DESCRIPTION: Creeping plant; purple stems, roundish, lobed, violet flowers in whorls. Gill-Over-Ground or ground ivy is available year around. Leaves may be dried and steeped in hot water for about ten minutes.

PHARMACEUTICAL USES: Tea used to treat measles. Chinese use to clear fever, dissolve stones in urinary tract, stimulate circulation, reduce inflammation, treat influenza, and alleviate pain.

HENBIT, DEAD NETTLE (Lamium purpureum) (502)

DESCRIPTION: Henbit looks like ground ivy, but is erect plant; small bugle like purple flowers in whorl. Found along fringe of fields and edges of yards.

COOKING TIPS: Young leaves and flowers may be added to salads. Cook the whole shoot in vegetable soups and stews.

POKEWEED (Phytolacca americana) (510)

DESCRIPTION: Large leaves; reddish, coarse stems, greenish white flowers in clusters, purple black berries on stalk. Pokeweed, or poke, found growing on waste ground almost anywhere in U.S. Very young leaves, as they first emerge, are edible after cooking in at least 2 changes of water. Root, stems, and berries of plant are poisonous.

WARNING: DON'T EAT POKE UNLESS FORAGING WITH BOTANIST.

PHARMACEUTICAL USES: Slightly narcotic, emetic and purgative. Berries used as poultice on wounds and sores. Seeds and fruits steeped in water, used to treat arthritis.

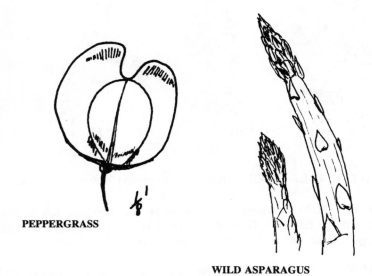

PEPPERGRASS

WILD ASPARAGUS

PEPPERGRASS (Lepidium virginicum) (550)

DESCRIPTION: Flat seed pods, peppery taste; lance-leaf, toothed. Add seeds to salads. Young leaves are edible ... but bitter, use sparingly.

PHARMACEUTICAL USES: Tea from leaves and seeds said to restore sex drive. Amerindians used plant as general medicinal.

WILD ASPARAGUS (Asparagus officinalis) (554)

DESCRIPTION: Plant green spike as first emerges. Found along roadsides and fence rows. Roadside plants may be tainted with benzene, lead, oil and other auto pollutants. Locate asparagus in the fall, when large, feathery, adult plants are easiest to see. Mark spot. Harvest the following spring.

COOKING TIPS: One favorite is asparagus roll-ups. Place 3 spears of asparagus on flour tortilla. Cover asparagus with cheddar cheese and Miracle Whip. Microwave tortilla for 35 seconds on high. Cover hot asparagus and cheese with bean sprouts, roll up tortilla ... GREAT!

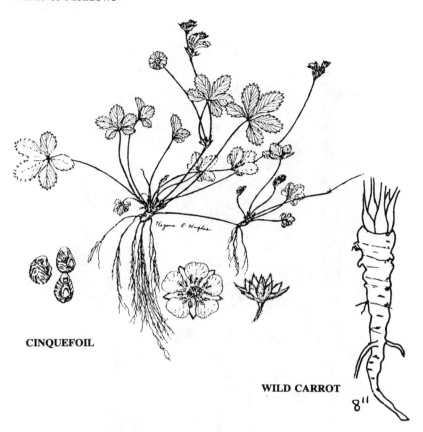

CINQUEFOIL

WILD CARROT

8"

CINQUEFOIL (Potentilla canadensis) (562)

DESCRIPTION: 5 to 7 long toothed leaflets; small, yellow-green flower. Found in yards, fields and waste ground.

CARROT, QUEEN ANNE'S LACE (Daucus carota) (569)

DESCRIPTION: A biennial, fine, deeply dissected leaf. Second year's growth has white flower many call Queen Anne's Lace. Root smells and tastes like domestic carrot, BUT IS TOUGH AND WOODY.

WARNING: BE CERTAIN, BEFORE USING WILD CARROT, THAT IT HAS CHARACTERISTIC CARROT SMELL ... HEMLOCK LOOK-ALIKE.

COOKING TIPS: Good in vegetable stew, imparts carrot flavor. Eat soft tissue around root's pithy core. High in Vitamin A and fiber.

BURDOCK

BURDOCK (Arctium minus) (580)

DESCRIPTION: Large leaf, looks like elephant ear; large taproot. Common garden nuisance. In June or July, dig first year roots of this biennial.

COOKING TIPS: Peel roots and cut into thin strips. Boil strips in water … If bitter, use two changes of water. Serve hot under a pat of butter and dollop of sour cream. Mock celery soup may be made with the young leaf steams of burdock. Add burdock, wild carrots and wild onions to chicken stock, cook, season and serve.

PHARMACEUTICAL USES: 18th century treatment for gonorrhea and syphilis. Amerindians used for scurvy, sores, rheumatism. Chinese use for tonsillitis, flu, as poultice on boils and abscesses.

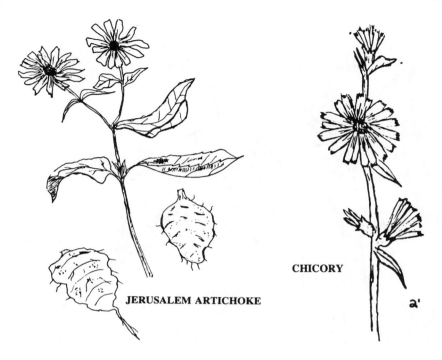

CHICORY

JERUSALEM ARTICHOKE

a'

JERUSALEM ARTICHOKE (Helianthus tuberosus) (595)

DESCRIPTION: Yellow sunflower; broad ovate, rough leaves, lower leaves opposite, upper leaves alternate, hairy stem, tuberous root. This plant may be found along roadsides. Add tubers to your garden, provides substantial food source that continues to reproduce year after year. Harvest tubers in fall, spring.

COOKING TIPS: Tuber may be sliced and eaten raw ... Has taste similar to water chestnut. Also microwave, bake, or boil like a potato. This plant is worth looking for.

CHICORY (Cichorium intybus) (610)

DESCRIPTION: Leaves lance shaped, deeply cut, dissected margins, stiff mid-vein spine; blue flower. Common along the shoulders of rural roads.

COOKING TIPS: Down New Orleans way dried root of chicory is ground and blended with coffee. Young leaves are edible, although bitter.

PHARMACEUTICAL USES: Occasionally used as a nerve tonic.

WEEPING WILLOW

WEEPING WILLOW (Salix Alba) (613)
SWAMP WILLOW (S. nigra)

DESCRIPTION: Tree or shrub; prefers wet ground, lance- like, fine toothed leaves. White or weeping willow and black willow, sometimes called marsh willow, have received much notoriety lately as a medicinal. Salicin from willow has anti-inflammatory action like aspirin.

PHARMACEUTICAL USES: Willow may be made from stems and leaves. Drop willow cuttings into hot water. Steep for one minute. Relaxing brew, that may take the edge off an aching head.

CAUTION: TOO MUCH SALICIN MAY BE DANGEROUS. CONSULT YOUR PHYSICIAN BEFORE TRYING THIS TEA.

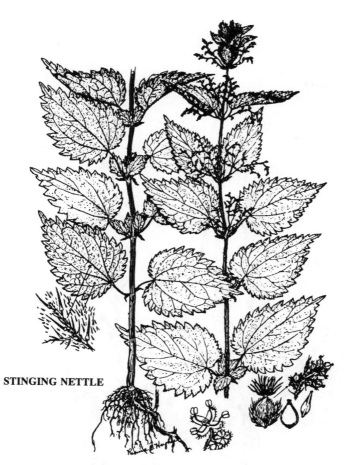

STINGING NETTLE

STINGING NETTLE (Urtica dioica) (630)

DESCRIPTION: Hairy stem and leaves; hairs sting, leaves lance-like, sharply toothed. Common resident along roadsides, fields and wooded areas. Fine stinging hairs contain skin irritant. Irritant is destroyed when plant is cooked.

COOKING TIPS: Cook with wild carrot, wild leeks, dandelion greens and soy sauce. Boil older plants, throw away the plants and use nettle stock for soups or as refreshing vitamin-rich drink.

CAUTION: DON'T CONFUSE THE HAIRY STINGING CELLS OF NETTLE WITH THE THORNY, POISONOUS HORSE NETTLE.

PHARMACEUTICAL USES: Tea may combat diarrhea. Diuretic in decoction. Herbalists rubbed whole plant over arthritic joints and muscles as counter-irritant.

MULLEIN

MULLEIN (Verbascum blattaria) (640)

DESCRIPTION: Large hairy, vel-cro like leaf; yellow flower, biennial, prostrate first year erect second year. Grows in vacant lots. Amerindians lined moccasins with the warm, woolly leaf.

PHARMACEUTICAL USES: Tea from leaves and flowers used to treat coughs, colds and bronchitis. Hairy leaves used to rub out pain of stinging nettle.

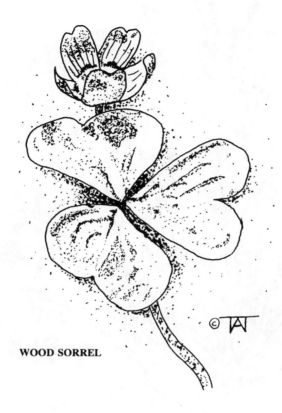

WOOD SORREL

WOOD SORREL (Oxalis montana) (647)

DESCRIPTION: Shamrock like leaf, deeply dissected into three round lobes; yellow flower. Wood sorrel (and related species: garden sorrel) leaves, flowers and seeds have a sour taste.

COOKING TIPS: Add yellow flowers, seeds and leaves to salads ... Or brew them into a beverage.

CAUTION: USE THIS PLANT SPARINGLY. EXCESSIVE CONSUMP-TION MAY INHIBIT ABSORPTION OF CALCIUM IN THE BODY.

PHARMACEUTICAL USES: Chinese use Oxalis species to clear fevers, resolve clots, and reduce swelling. Also, used as snake bite treatment.

SHEEP SORREL

SHEEP SORREL (Rumex acetoscella) (653)

DESCRIPTION: Thick, succulent leaves, long pointed, tapered tip, with short, pointed basal lobes. Leaves taste sour. Found on waste ground, wood margins, gardens. Available spring and fall.

COOKING TIPS: Prepare like wood sorrel. Eat sparingly.

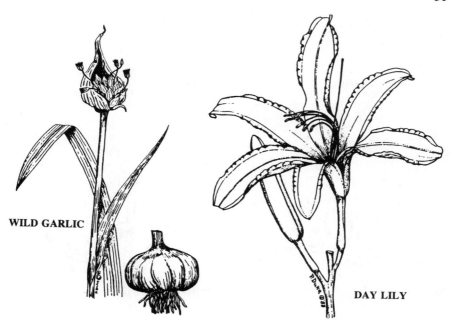

WILD GARLIC

DAY LILY

WILD GARLIC (Allium sativum) (660)

DESCRIPTION: Long, narrow, pencil-like leaf stalk, flower head bears small green "plantlets" that drop off and propagate.

PHARMACEUTICAL USES: Wild garlic, chives, onions may reduce blood pressure, lower cholesterol, lower blood sugar.

DAY LILY (Hemerocallis fulva) (665)

DESCRIPTION: Yellow, tuberous roots; narrow, long lance-like leaves, orange lily flower. Found along roadsides. Transplant to clean soil away from auto pollution.

COOKING TIPS: Add strong tasting flowers to summer salads. Buds may be steamed, boiled or deep fried ... Serve with butter or cheese sauce. Firm root tubers may be harvested all year. Add raw to salads or cook like a potato.

CAUTION: USE PLANT WHEN IN BLOOM ... EARLY GROWTH RESEMBLES POISONOUS IRIS SHOOTS, YELLOWISH TUBERS ARE DISTINCTIVE.

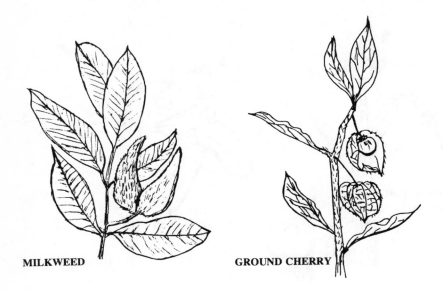

MILKWEED   GROUND CHERRY

MILKWEED (Asclepias syriaca) (677)

DESCRIPTION: White sticky sap; large, egg-like seed pods, large ovate leaves. Common milkweed is sometimes eaten as cooked vegetable. But the sap contains toxins. Cattle and sheep have died from milkweed poisoning. Don't eat this plant.

COOKING TIPS: DO NOT EAT THIS PLANT.

PHARMACEUTICAL USES: Sap used to treat warts, moles and ringworm. Boiled roots used to treat sterility, asthma and dysentery.

GROUND CHERRY, LANTERN PLANT (Physalis pubescense) (680)

DESCRIPTION: Hairy stems and leaves; pale green plant ... Sometimes called lantern plant, because of the lantern like husk. Ground cherries may be harvested when ripe, usually August or September.

COOKING TIPS: UNRIPE BERRIES may make you sick. Like other members of the nightshade family, best avoid this fruit.

PHARMACEUTICAL USES: Used by Chinese as poultice over abscesses, vermicide, cough sedative.

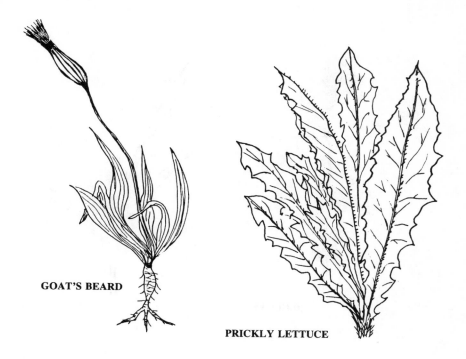

GOAT'S BEARD

PRICKLY LETTUCE

GOAT'S BEARD (Tragopogon pratensis) (688)

DESCRIPTION: Goat's beard looks like a large dandelion. It has a yellow flower. Large, deeply, sharply serrated leaves like dandelion.

COOKING TIPS: Root edible; boiled, then fried.

PHARMACEUTICAL USES: Apply cooled infusion of plant to boils ... Also, gargled for sore throat treatment.

PRICKLY LETTUCE (Lactuca scariola) (691)

DESCRIPTION: Lettuce-like; white, sticky juice in stems, leaves; leaves alternate, lance-like, toothed and spiny margin; small yellow flowers in clusters.

COOKING TIPS: Blanched leaves are bitter. Definitely won't impress dinner guests.

PHARMACEUTICAL USES: Was used as cough suppressant. About 200 years ago distilled scariola and "wild opium" (Lactuca canadensis) was very weak opium-like sedative.

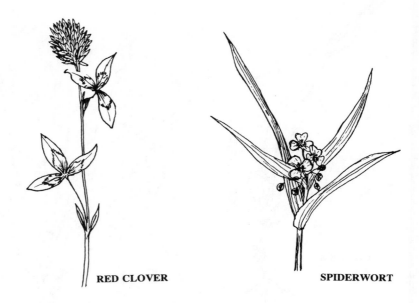

RED CLOVER   SPIDERWORT

RED CLOVER (Trifolium pratense) (695)

DESCRIPTION: Often three leaflets showing pale chevron; round flower head, rose purple flower petals that may be eaten raw in salads or batter fried.

PHARMACEUTICAL USES: Skilled herbalists used this plant to treat cuts, burns, and treat liver ailments.

SPIDERWORT (Tradescantia virginiana) (702)

DESCRIPTION: Flower violet, 3 round petals, long golden stamens; long lanced leaves, common along roadsides. Young shoots and leaves may be eaten, but are mucilaginous ... Or as my daughter puts it, "They're slimy!"

COOKING TIPS: Floral salad, strong tasting.

PHARMACEUTICAL USES: Poulticed root rubbed on skin cancer. Tea for stomach ache.

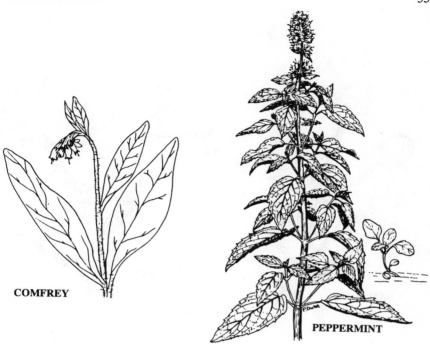

COMFREY

PEPPERMINT

COMFREY (Symphytum officinale) (708)

DESCRIPTION: Leaves large, elongated, hairy, prickly; stalks hollow hairy, flower, finger-like, pale white. Found on moist low ground.

COOKING TIPS: Eat raw or cooked.

WARNING: THIS PLANT MAY BE CARCINOGENIC.

PHARMACEUTICAL USES: Plant parts demulcent, astringent. Amerindians used tea for dysentery, gonorrhea, and heartburn.

PEPPERMINT (Mentha piperita) (713)

DESCRIPTION: Peppermint, like spearmint, found along wet lowlands, streams and lakes. It has a square stem, like most members of the mint family, with opposite leaves, sharply serrated. Crushed plant has strong aromatic odor of mint.

COOKING TIPS: Flowers in salads. Leaves flavor cold drinks, teas.

PHARMACEUTICAL USES: Oil used to treat colic. Tea used to treat colds, fever and headache.

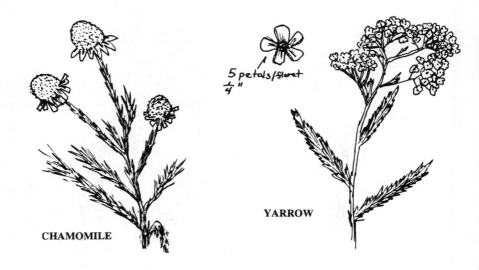

CHAMOMILE (Anthemis nobilis) (not in video)

DESCRIPTION: Aromatic; hairy stem, narrow leaflets divided into many segments, flower on long, erect stem, yellow/white florets, sandy soil, full sun.

PHARMACEUTICAL USES: Flower makes excellent tea — soothing, relaxing brew, sometimes taken for indigestion. Available over-the-counter.

CAUTION: OVER-DOSAGE MAY CAUSE VOMITING. SIMILAR TO RAGWEED POLLEN MAY TRIGGER ALLERGIES.

YARROW, MILFOIL (Achillea millefolium) (not in video)

DESCRIPTION: Aromatic; creeping or erect herb, leaves feather-like, slightly hairy, divided into fine leaflets, white or pinkish flower. Found in open sun or partial shade.

PHARMACEUTICAL USES: Was used as poultice over wounds. Tea used to treat colds.

WARNING: YARROW LOOKS SIMILAR TO POISONOUS HEMLOCK. GET EXPERT IDENTIFICATION.

Woodlands

HEPATICA

HEPATICA, AM. LIVERWORT (Anemone hepatica) (749)

DESCRIPTION: Perennial plant; leaves on long hairy petiole, shaped like 3 lobes of liver, flower appears early, white, blue or purplish. One of first flowers to bloom in MARCH or APRIL.

PHARMACEUTICAL USES: Small amounts of roots and leaves used to treat indigestion, disorders of the kidneys, gall bladder, and liver.

CAUTION: LARGE AMOUNTS OF HEPATICA ARE POISONOUS. USE IS RESERVED FOR A SKILLED HERBALIST.

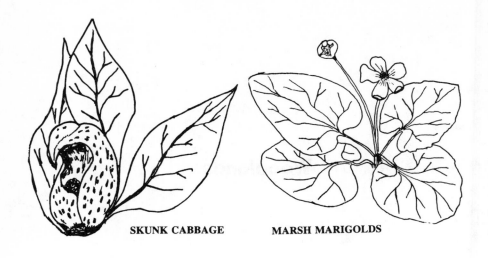

SKUNK CABBAGE   MARSH MARIGOLDS

SKUNK CABBAGE (Symplocarpus foetidus) (754)

DESCRIPTION: Plant smells like a skunk when damaged; leaves large, smooth margins; primitive spathe (flower) emerges before leaves. The plant is found in wet lowlands and woods.

PHARMACEUTICAL USES: Roots used as medicinal. First, were thoroughly dried to crystallize burning oxalate. Infusion or tea from the dried root used mild sedative.

CAUTION: PLANT IS POISONOUS. JUICE FROM THE FRESH PLANT MAY CAUSE SKIN BLISTERING AND SEVERELY BURN DIGESTIVE TRACT IF EATEN. ONLY EXPERTS SHOULD HANDLE THIS PLANT.

MARSH MARIGOLDS, COWSLIP (Caltha palustris) (769)

DESCRIPTION: Leaves ovate; plants grow in low, WETLANDS, flower bright yellow. Fluorescent yellow flowers of Marsh Marigolds are distinctive. Thrives in sunlight to partial shade.

COOKING TIPS: Leaves eaten as a potherb in the spring before the flowers open … But this is a risky practice. They must be cooked in several changes of water because they are extremely bitter. Not worth time and trouble.

CAUTION: IN VIEW OF THE CAUSTIC NATURE OF THIS PLANT, BEST AVOID IT.

PHARMACEUTICAL USES: Leaves used as laxative and cough syrup. Root in decoction for colds.

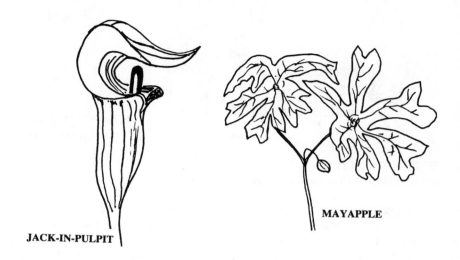

JACK-IN-PULPIT

MAYAPPLE

JACK-IN-PULPIT, INDIAN TURNIP (Arisaema triphyllum) (772)

DESCRIPTION: Leaves compound, three leaflets, oval, smooth lighter underside; distinctive primitive flower, spadix in pulpit-like spathe. Indian Turnip is found in rich soils, generally a woods, or shady lowland. Like skunk cabbage, this plant contains calcium oxalate and is not edible raw.

COOKING TIPS: Amerindians sliced roots and dried them, deactivating calcium oxalate. Dried root was cooked, and eaten like potato chips.

PHARMACEUTICAL USES: Plant parts used in treatment of cough, sorethroat and ringworm. Also, as a poultice for boils and abscesses.

MAYAPPLE (Podophyllum peltatum) (782)

DESCRIPTION: Large pair of dissected, parasol-like leaves, white flower on petiole between leaves, yellow/green fruit. Mayapple is, for the most part, poisonous. The two large parasol like leaves shelter a white flower that bears an edible fruit when ripe in mid-summer. Pick the fruit when soft and ripe.

COOKING TIPS: Expert foragers carefully gather ripe fruit for use in pie fillings and jellies.

REMEMBER, this plant is poisonous, except the pulp of the ripe fruits.

PHARMACEUTICAL USES: Etoposide, active agent of Mayapple may be useful treating testicular and small lung cancer.

 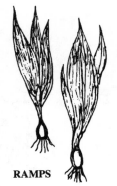 

6" TRILLIUM

RAMPS   FIDDLEHEAD FERNS

WHITE TRILLIUM (Trillium grandiflorum) (828)
TOADSHADE (Trillim cuneatum) (828)

   DESCRIPTION: Leaves, sepals and flower petals in threes. There are several varieties of trillium. Leaves and flowers are edible. But for my taste members of this genus are too pretty to eat.
   Trillium and toadshade are excellent transplants. Get permission from land owner, then dig up the entire plant with at least an EIGHT inch earthball. Locate in shade and rich soil.

RAMPS, WILD LEEKS (Allium tricoccum) (837)

   DESCRIPTION: Strong onion aroma; long, wide leaves grow directly from bulb. Ramps are found on banks, wet woods — premium quality food!

   COOKING TIPS: Leaves stems and bulbs are edible: marvelous in stews, and soup, or simply sauteed in the wilds. Simply add soy sauce. Some EXTRA VIRGIN olive oil. And a little water to keep plants from sticking to pan.

   PHARMACEUTICAL USES: Used as a tonic, combats colds. Disputed evidence that eating raw bulbs may reduce risk of heart disease.

FIDDLEHEAD FERNS (Matteucia and Pteretis) (845)

   DESCRIPTION: Early growth of fern, tightly wound like a fiddlehead. Fiddleheads are the unfurled leaves of ferns.

   COOKING TIPS: They may be eaten raw, or steamed. I prefer them sauteed or deep fried.

   CAUTION: SOME FERNS SUCH AS BRACKEN FERN MAY CAUSE STOMACH CANCER. FIDDLEHEADS MAY ALSO LEAD TO THIAMINE PROBLEMS. BEST AVOID THESE PLANTS.

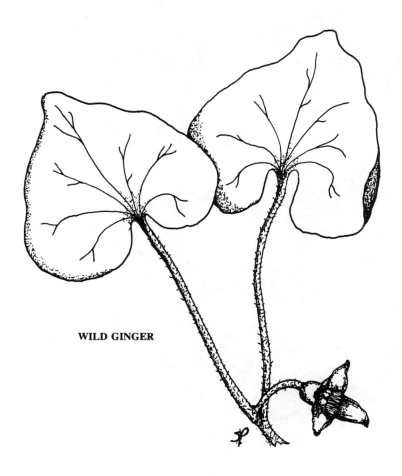

WILD GINGER

WILD GINGER (Asarum canadense) (850)

DESCRIPTION: Aromatic root, smells like ginger; two heart shaped leaves, petioles and primitive flower hairy. Note the hairy stem and heart shaped leaves. In May, the primitive flower emerges. Found on rich soil in moist woods.

COOKING TIPS: Crushed root added to salad dressings. When dried and grated it is an adequate substitute for oriental ginger. For the daring gourmet, try boiling the root until tender ... Then simmer in maple syrup, an UNUSUAL candy treat.

PHARMACEUTICAL USES: Root was used to treat colds and cough, antiseptic and tonic.

SWEET CICELY

SWEET CICELY, WILD ANISE (Myrrhis odorata) (858)

DESCRIPTION: WARNING: LOOKS LIKE HEMLOCK. Broken root smell like anise. Bright green, shiny leaves; small, white flowers in umbels. Wild anise, commonly called sweet cicely, has a sweet anise odor and taste. Use as an anis substitute.

COOKING TIPS: Use root to spice cooked greens.

PHARMACEUTICAL USES: Leaves occasionally eaten by diabetics as sugar substitute.

42

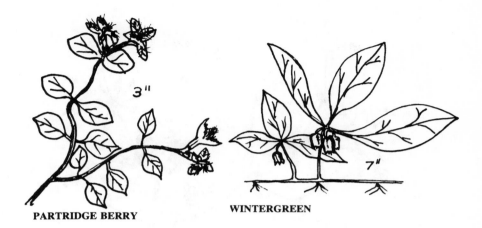

PARTRIDGE BERRY   WINTERGREEN

PARTRIDGE BERRY (Mitchella repens) (865)

DESCRIPTION: A tiny creeper, with oval leaves, found at the base of trees in wet woods of the northern and central U.S. and Canada. Bland berry ripens to bright red by late-summer.

COOKING TIPS: A tasteless trail food, with little or no bulk — a hard times, survival berry, available all winter.

WINTERGREEN (Gaultheria procumbens) (879)

DESCRIPTION: Long oval leaves, finely serrated margins; evergreen, drooping white flowers. There are several species of this plant in North America. Creeping wintergreen, or checkerberry is found in the Eastern half of the U.S. The flower forms an edible berry that turns from white to red by late summer … Available all winter — if not gobbled up by late season foragers.

COOKING TIPS: Add summer fruits to pancake and muffin mixes. Leaves make a delicate tea, or munch them (don't swallow) as a breath freshener.

PHARMACEUTICAL USES: Astringent and counterirritant. Never take oil internally, poisonous. Tea from leaves has been used for flu, colds and stomach alkalizer.

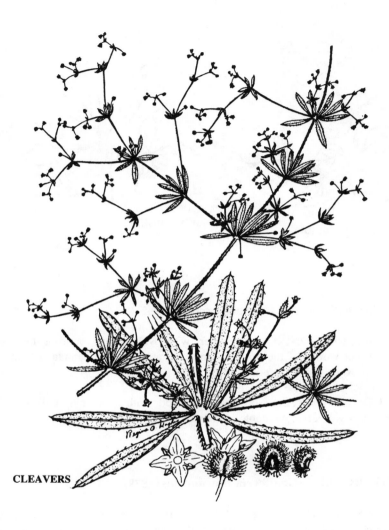

CLEAVERS

CLEAVERS, GOOSEGRASS (Galium aparine) (886)

DESCRIPTION: Slender, weak stem; 8 leaves in whorl, tiny white flowers. Found in woodlands, along streams and in vacant lots.

COOKING TIPS: Also called Bedstraw, cleaver leaves may be added to salads in early spring, but tough, mature leaves must be cooked. Seeds of summer may be roasted and ground into coffee substitute. It's better than chicory but far short of coffee.

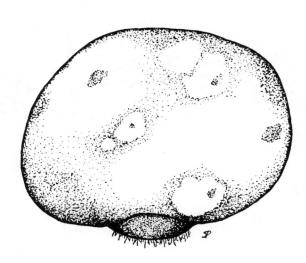

GREY MOREL

PUFFBALL MUSHROOM

GREY MOREL MUSHROOM (Morchella esculenta) (890) 86
BLACK MOREL (Morchella spp.) (892)

DESCRIPTION: Convoluted, brain-like flesh, grey or black. Found from about mid-April through May, in many wooded areas of the U.S. ... Convoluted brain look is distinctive, but there are some dangerous look-alikes.

WARNING: MANY MUSHROOMS ARE DEADLY. SEEK POSITIVE IDENTIFICATION FROM AN EXPERT BEFORE EATING.

PUFFBALL MUSHROOM (Calvatea gigantea) (897)

DESCRIPTION: Large, football to basketball sized mushroom, white, fleshy white throughout. Puffball is found on rich soil in shady areas. It may be cooked like an edible mushroom. Before eating, cut open and be certain flesh is white and not yellow. Also, avoid this plant if gills or a rudimentary stem are inside.

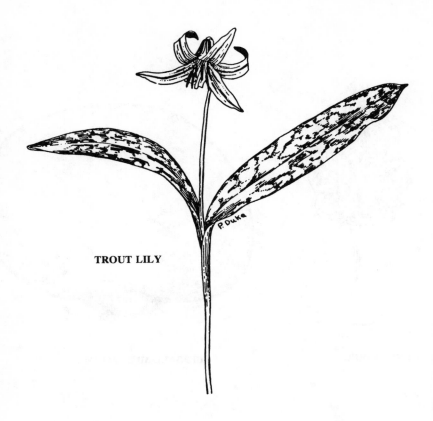

TROUT LILY

TROUT LILY (Erythronium americanum) (901)

DESCRIPTION: Trout Lily or dog toothed violet has mottled leaves and small yellow lily-like flower.

COOKING TIPS: Young leaves may be boiled for 10 minutes and eaten, poor tasting. The tuberous root is also edible ... after lengthy boiling. The real beauty of this plant is in the eyes of the beholder ... As a foodstuff it's best left alone.

PHARMACEUTICAL USES: Tea from root used to reduce fever. Crushed leaves used as poultice over ulcers.

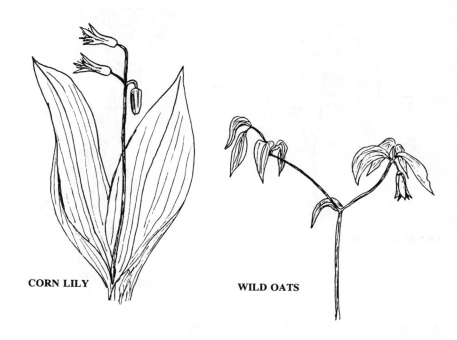

CORN LILY   WILD OATS

CORN LILY (Clintonia borealis) (not in video)

DESCRIPTION: Near look-alike of trout lily. Has waxy leaves ... Is edible ... But like the trout lily, it's best to leave this inferior foodstuff alone.

PHARMACEUTICAL USES: Amerindians used leaves as poultice over wounds, sores and burns. Tea from root used as mosquito repellent.

WILD OATS (Uvularia sassilifolia (907)

DESCRIPTION: Yellow, drooping, lily-like flower; angled stem, leaves do not surround stem as in related bellwort species.
The early spring shoots of Wild Oats may be eaten ... But use them sparingly. Avoid picking this plant where not abundant.

PHARMACEUTICAL USES: Root used as poultice over boils and wounds. Boiled root used to treat diarrhea.

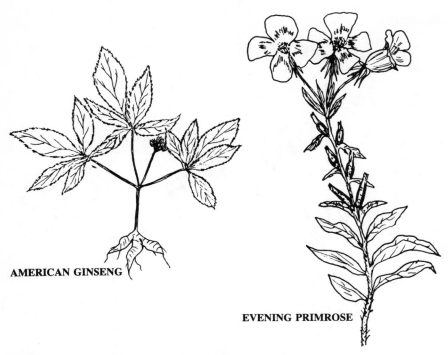

AMERICAN GINSENG

EVENING PRIMROSE

AMERICAN GINSENG (Panax quinquifolius) (918)

DESCRIPTION: Straight, erect stem, with 2 or 3 leaf stems; 5-11 leaves per stem. American Genseng root, a prized medicinal in China, sells for about $150 per pound. Commercially cultivated.

COOKING TIPS: Chinese cook root in chicken soup. They also eat berries.

PHARMACEUTICAL USES: Ginseng root's active ingredients, called saponins (glycosides). Some saponins raise blood pressure, others lower it. Some raise blood sugar, some lower it. Obviously, more research is needed.

EVENING PRIMROSE (Oenothera biennis) (922)

DESCRIPTION: Yellow flower; biennial, second year erect plant, leaves lance shaped, pointed tip, fine toothed margin. Evening Primrose, is found in fields bordering wooded areas. The flowers, roots and seeds are edible.

COOKING TIPS: Dip flowers in egg whites. Roll them in sugar. Then deep fry.

PHARMACEUTICAL USES: Plant parts contain Gamma Linolenic Acid (GLA). GLA may prevent acne, alcoholism, obesity and schizophrenia (as yet unproven).

48

GROUND NUT

GROUND NUT (Apios americana) (932)

DESCRIPTION: Pea-like plant; numerous tubers along root, leaves alternate, compound featherlike, seeds in long pod. Ground nut grows on wet ground, along the fringes of streams, bogs and thickets. It's a climbing pea-like vine, developing numerous tubers along the length of its root.

COOKING TIPS: Seeds are edible. Cook them like lentils. Tubers of Apios are 15% protein, a great potato substitute.

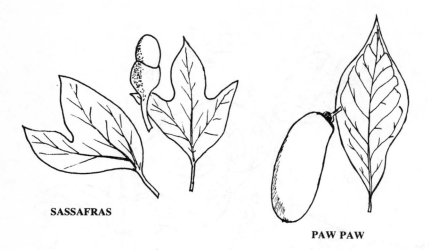

SASSAFRAS

PAW PAW

SASSAFRAS (Sasafras albidum) (944)

DESCRIPTION: Small tree with aromatic limbs, leaves and roots. Decoctions from root was used as a tea substitute during colonial times. The leaves usually have two or three lobes, are alternate. There are many sucker plants growing adventitously from the parent plant.

COOKING TIPS: Boil root, sweeten and drink.

PHARMACEUTICAL USES: Sassafras tea used as a diuretic and stimulant. Leaves and bark made into a tea and rubbed on the body may work as a mosquito repellent.

CAUTION: SASSAFRAS OILS MAY BE CARCINOGENIC.

PAW PAW (Asimina triloba) (946)

DESCRIPTION: Small tree (10' to 25') growing on river banks, along streams, often a secondary growth under taller trees. Leaves are alternate, simple, large (up to 12") narrow at base broad near tip.

COOKING TIPS: Large fruit eaten raw. Or remove seeds, cook like pudding, blend with yogurt.

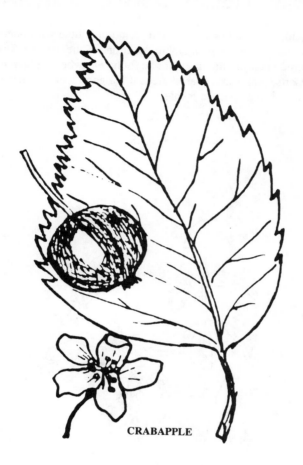

CRABAPPLE

APPLE, CRABAPPLE (Malus, Pyrus spp) (950)

DESCRIPTION: Wild apples, pears, crabapples small trees to 30'. Some species have thorns. Flowers white, rosy white, smaller than domestic apples.

COOKING TIPS: Sour, acid taste, cook with sugar or honey. Make preserve with raspberries, blueberries, or blackberries.

PHARMACEUTICAL USES: Fruit cooked, eaten for colds.

Mountains, Plaines, Deserts, Seacoasts

This section identifies a few of the more common edible wild plants found in unique environments. Each geographic location in the United States and Canada has endemic plant life that may not be found elsewhere. When traveling in mountains, deserts, plains and coastal areas it's a good idea to pack along an edible plants book for that specific locale.

MOUNTAINS

JOJOBA

JOJOBA (Simmondsia californica)

DESCRIPTION: Southwestern U.S., mountains, desert/mountain borders. Shrub. Seed capsules burst in early fall disgorging oily, chocolate colored seeds. Seeds are eaten.

COOKING TIPS: Seeds eaten raw or cooked. Roasted and ground seeds are whipped in cooked egg yolks until paste forms. Boil in milk, sugar and a little water. Add a drop or two of vanilla extract to flavor ... Drink hot.

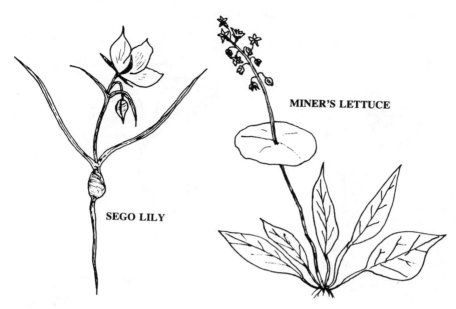

SEGO LILY (Calochortus gunnisonii)

DESCRIPTION: Found below timberline in meadows, open slopes. Blade-like leaves, flowers vary white with purple spots to orange and red (use color photographs for identification). Pick early, above ground part of plant disappears in July.

COOKING TIPS: Bulb is reported as edible. Roast or boil. Mash like potato. Author does not recommend eating this plant, unless foraging with a knowledgeable expert.

WARNING: DO NOT CONFUSE THIS PLANT WITH DEATH CAMAS. GET PROFESSIONAL, EXPERT IDENTIFICATION.

MINER'S LETTUCE (Montia perfoliata)

DESCRIPTION: Leaves form cup or saucer around stems; delicate, small white flowers. Found in moist, shady places ... Pacific coastal range, east to plains.

COOKING TIPS: Eat leaves and stems raw. Or cook like dandelion greens. High in Vitamin A. Best with vinegar-laced salad dressing. Reportedly, Amerindians used ant waste (acidic waste products of digestive tract) to flavor miner's lettuce. Sugar water placed over greens attracts ants that eliminate waste products over leaves.

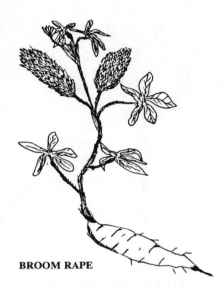

INDIAN BREAD ROOT   **BROOM RAPE**

INDIAN BREAD ROOT, PRAIRIE TURNIP (Psoralea esculenta)

DESCRIPTION: Low lying, hairy herbs of the prairie; long stemmed leaves, compound, divided into five fingers, flowers in dense, blue spike, each floret looks like small pea blossom. Edible part is 1" to 2" tuberous root.

COOKING TIPS: Eat raw, sliced in salad with vinegar and oil dressing. Roots may be dried and preserved. Add dried root to soups, stews.

PHARMACEUTICAL USES: High in starch, may be 70% starch. Psoralea genus used to treat psoriasis (PUVA) and some forms of cancer (Psoralen/photo-phoresis).

BROOM RAPE (Orobanche fasciculata)

DESCRIPTION: Parasitic plants of plains and western hillsides. Color yellow to brown, similar to squaw root. Scale-like alternating leaves rising up stem. Flowers irregular, bellshaped.

COOKING TIPS: Amerindians ate whole plant roasted in hot ashes. The author has not eaten this plant. I recommend you do not eat it unless with an absolute authority; and expert botanist who has prepared Broom Rape.

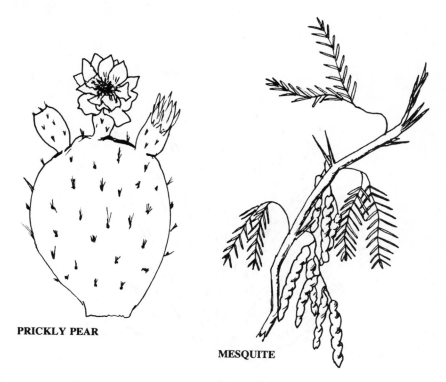

PRICKLY PEAR

MESQUITE

PRICKLY PEAR, INDIAN FIG (Opuntia humifusa)

DESCRIPTION: Dryland, desert cactus, sandy soil. Spreads along ground. Has broad but thin fleshy segments, spined. Segments are pear shaped but flattened, fruit is pear-shaped, rounded. Flower yellow blooms in March and April.

COOKING TIPS: Harvest carefully, wear gloves. Peel or flame away spines. Slice "leaf" into segments, then stir fry, deep fry, or roast over open fire. Pulp of ripe fruit may be removed and made into jelly.

MESQUITE (Prosopis juliflora)

DESCRIPTION: Woody tree or shrub of arid regions. Leaves compound, featherlike. Seed pods resemble green bean pods.

COOKING TIPS: Wood used to cook and flavor meats. Seed pods edible, juicy, sweet when ripe, very seedy.

CAREFUL: MAY CAUSE DERMATITIS ON SOME INDIVIDUALS.

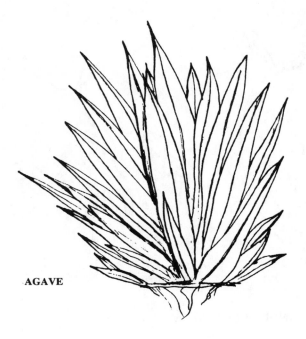

AGAVE

AGAVE, CENTURY PLANT, MESCAL (Amaryllis sp.)

DESCRIPTION: Long sword-like, stiff, fibrous leaves, shooting skyward in a circular cluster. Huge flower stalk grows from leaf cradle to about 10' to 15' tall. Clusters of yellow flowers.

COOKING TIPS: Young bud of plant may be cut out. You may need help from the local native population to prepare the plant correctly. Bud must not be too old. Cut entire bud from leaves as it emerges. Trim away leaves and flower tips. Prepare fire in large pit lined with stones. Let large fire burn down to coals. Then put bud in ashes. Cover bud with hot stones and ashes, bury in dirt. Open the pit and recover the cooked bud 10 to 12 hours later. Cut away charred covering to expose sticky, sweet, pineapple tasting interior.

PHARMACEUTICAL USES: Plant fruit is made into native drink, Mescal.

SEASHORE TIDAL AREAS

Almost all marine seaweeds are safe to consume. Two questionable varieties, easy to avoid, are the foul tasting LYNGBYA, a thin, hairlike species that clings to mangrove roots in warm waters. The other, called DESMARESTIA, contains sulphuric acid and imparts an unpleasant lemon-like taste. Desmarestia is usually found in deep, open waters. Therefore, avoid mangrove clinging seaweeds and deep open water varieties.

Because of limited space only three popular edible seaweeds are covered, by no means the limit of your foraging choices. For more information on edible seaweeds get: *Sea Vegetables, Harvesting Guide and Cookbook,* by McConnaughey, Naturegraph; and *The Sea Vegetable Book,* Madlener, Potter.

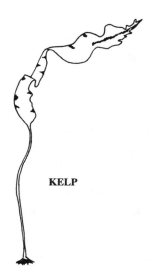

KELP

KELP (Laminaria sp.)

DESCRIPTION: A brown seaweed that may grow to over 100 feet in length. Large frond-like leaves, stem may be thick as a human's wrist, air filled bulbs or bladders hold plant erect in water. Plant is often torn loose and washed ashore after storms.

COOKING TIPS: Wash the plant in clean water. Soak in weak wine vinegar or lemon juice until pliable. Air dry in sun. After drying scrape off blue-green surface layer. Thick white core may be chopped, shredded or ground. Best cooked in soups and stews. Dry shredded parts for later use.

PHARMACEUTICAL USES: Improves yolk color when fed to chickens. Excellent fiber, good source of iodine. Important clotting agent. Kelp salt prevents muscle cramps.

NORI

ALARIA

NORI, LAVER, PORPHYRA (Porphyra sp.)

DESCRIPTION: Rose pink to red brown with aging. Flat, blade-like, irregular shape to 20". Satin sheen, thin, elastic. Found in mid-tidal zone.

COOKING TIPS: Forage in late spring. Sun dry, then store in canning jars, or plastic bags, airtight, no moisture. Use it fresh seasoned and tenderized in soy sauce. Dry and flake into baked goods. In soups and stews.

PHARMACEUTICAL USES: Nearly 36% protein. High in iodine. High in Vitamin A and C. May lower blood cholesterol levels, as yet unproven.

ALARIA, WAKAME (Alaria marginata)

DESCRIPTION: Olive brown to green. To 6 feet tall. Attached by short stem (stipe) and holdfast cell. Short paddle-like sporophylls just below edible frond blades. DO NOT CUT AWAY SPOROPHYLLS WHEN HARVESTING — this procedure guarantees the life and future of your Alaria supply. Found on rocks in lower tidal zones.

COOKING TIPS: Dry plant. May be restored with water to near fresh condition. Wrap reconstituted alaria leaves around rice and meats, cook in casseroles. Great in mushroom soup. Simmer in pot roast. Especially good when used in chicken soups and stews.

PHARMACEUTICAL USES: High in essential trace elements. Good source of pantothenic acid, Vitamin C and B vitamins.

Poisonous Plants

What follows is only a partial listing of poisonous plants in the United States. For a more comprehensive discussion refer to the books listed at the end of this chapter. Always keep the phone number of your poison control center at hand, in your wallet and your car.

100.   **AMERICAN LIVERWORT (Hepatica americana)** has kidney- or liver-shaped leaves with hairy petioles; first flower of spring. BURNING ALKALOID, REQUIRES SPECIAL PREPARATION FOR CONSUMPTION. USE RESERVED FOR SKILLED PHARMACIST OR HERBALIST.

101.   **ARROW ARUM (Peltandra virginica)** has arrow shaped leaf, pinnate veins; green primitive flower, grows in water. Some argue the burning alkaloids may be dried out of the seeds and roots. Even so, the bitter taste of the prepared plant is unfit to eat. ALL PARTS OF THIS PLANT, INCLUDING THE FLOWER AND MATURE FRUITS, ARE POISONOUS.

102.   **BLOODROOT (Sanguinaria canadensis)** has an underground rhizome that exudes a red "sap" when broken. Plant has a single, deeply dissected leaf, single white flower. Juice of plant is skin and eye irritant. EATING MODERATE QUANTITIES MAY BE FATAL.

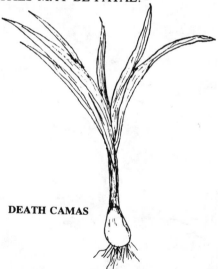

DEATH CAMAS

103.   **DEATH CAMAS, POISON SEGO (Zigadenus spp.)** is a sego lily look-alike. It grows 1.5' high, grasslike, yellow or white flowers growing along central flower stalk. Has onion-like bulb but no onion-like odor. All parts toxic. MAY CAUSE VOMITING, HEADACHE, DIZZINESS AND CONVULSIONS.

104.   **DUTCHMAN'S BREECHES (Dicentra cucullaria)** has deeply dissected, carrot-like leaves; white flower looks like "bloomers" or man's breeches. TUBER MOST POISONOUS. CAUSES CONVULSIONS AND BREATHING DIFFICULTIES ... RARELY FATAL.

105.   **HELLEBORE, FALSE (Veratrum viride)** has large ovate, stalkless leaves, clinging and spiraling up sturdy stem; flowers yellow-green, in branched clusters. Grows in wet, swampy areas. Western variety of hellebore grows on open mountain slopes. MAY CAUSE ASPHYXIA, CONVULSIONS AND DEATH.

106.   **HEMLOCK, POISON (Conium maculatum)** has purple spotted stems; large plant, white flowers in many branched flower heads (umbels). Be careful, many edible look-alikes such as: parsley, carrot, wild anise, parsnips and other members of the carrot family look like poison hemlock. TOXIN, CONINE, CAUSES RESPIRATORY FAILURE AND DEATH.

HORSE NETTLE

107.   **HORSE NETTLE (Solanum carolinense)** has spiny stems and leaves; leaves coarse, irregular large toothed; flower white; fruit fleshy yellow berry. ALKALOID, SOLANUM, CAUSES NAUSEA, VOMITING, STOMACH AND BOWEL PAIN.

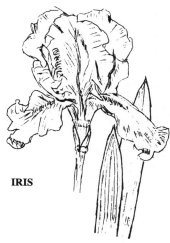

IRIS

108.   **IRIS, BLUE FLAG (Iris spp.)** has sword-like leaves; purple, blue or yellow flower, rhizome. CAUSES DIARRHEA, VOMITING AND DERMATITIS.

109.   **JACK-IN-THE-PULPIT (Arisaema triphyllum)** flower has characteristic spathe and spadix ... like preacher in a pulpit. BURNING CALCIUM OXALATE CRYSTALS WHEN EATEN FRESH.

110.   **JIMSON WEED, DATURA (Datura stramonium)** large plant; spiny stems, spiny fruit pod, spined leaves and spiny flower. HALLUCINATIONS, DELIRIUM AND VIOLENT ACTIONS RESULT FROM EATING PLANT PARTS. RARELY FATAL.

111.   **MAYAPPLE (Podophyllum peltatum)** plant of the woods; leaf parasol-like, deeply dissected, single white flower; yellow/green fruit. SERIOUS CASES OF PLANT INGESTION MAY LEAD TO COMA AND DEATH.

112.   **MILKWEED (Asclepsias spp.)** large ovate leaves; stomach-shaped fruit pod; plants exude milk-like sap when damaged. OVERDOSE OF GALITOXIN (MILKWEED TOXIN) HAS CAUSED DEATH IN LIVESTOCK.

113.   **NIGHTSHADE, BITTERSWEET NIGHTSHADE (Solanum dulcamara)** is a climbing vine, with purple rocket shaped flowers, bearing a red fruit. Leaves lobed, alternate. RARELY FATAL.

114.   **POISON IVY (Toxicodendren [Rhus] radicans)** climbing vine or shrub; hairy stem, leaflets in threes, white or pale yellow berries. CONTACT MAY CAUSE DERMATITIS.

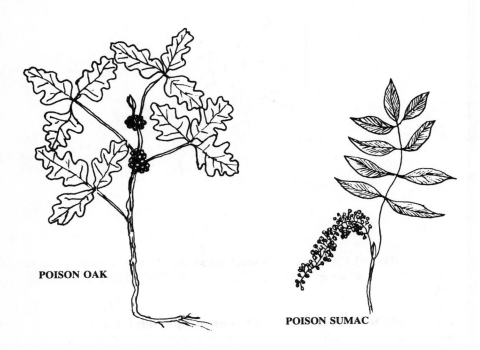

POISON OAK

POISON SUMAC

115.   **POISON OAK (Toxicodendren pubescens)** small shrub; resembles poison ivy, leaves more lobed. CONTACT CAUSES DERMATITIS.

116.   **POISON SUMAC (Rhus vernix)** is a shrub with compound leaves; 7-15 leaflets, white fruits instead of red fruit of sumac. CAUSES DERMATITIS.

117.   **POKEWEED (Phytolacca americana)** ovate leaves, pointed at tip; reddish, purple stems, clusters of fruit, purple-red colored ... grows on wasteland. RARELY FATAL ... CAN CAUSE CRAMPS AND VOMITING.

118.   **SKUNK CABBAGE (Symplocarpus foetidus)** is wetlands dweller; primitive fleshy plant, large ovate leaves, plant smells like skunk when torn or damaged, primitive flower (spadix and spathe). RARELY FATAL, TERRIBLE BURNING, BITTER TASTE.

119.   **WATERHEMLOCK (Cicuta maculata)** inhabits wetlands. Has sharply toothed leaves, similar to poison hemlock in appearance, looks like many edible members of carrot family ... BEWARE. CONVULSIONS AND DEATH A FEW HOURS AFTER CONSUMPTION.

*USEFUL REFERENCES: *100 Poisonous Plants of Maryland,* Steven Hill, and Peggy Duke, Bulletin 314, University of Maryland, Cooperative Extension Service, 1986.

Poisonous Plants of United States, Muenscher, W. C., Collier Books, NY, NY 1975.

AMA Handbook of Poisonous and Injurious Plants, by Lampe and McCann, AMA, Chicago, IL.

INDEX